15-MINUTE MINDFUL MEALS

250+ FAIL-PROOF RECIPES AND IDEAS FOR QUICK, PLEASURABLE & HEALTHY HOME COOKING

Caleb Warnock & Lori Henderson

THE BACKYARD RENAISSANCE COLLECTION

DISCOVER THE LONG-LOST SKILLS OF SELF-RELIANCE

My name is Caleb Warnock, and I've been working for years to learn how to return to forgotten skills, the skills of our ancestors. As our world becomes increasingly unstable, self-reliance becomes invaluable. Throughout this series, *Backyard Renaissance*, I will share with you the lost skills of self-sufficiency and healthy living. Come with me and other do-it-yourself experimenters, and rediscover the joys and success of simple self-reliance.

FAMILIUS

Copyright © 2016 by Caleb Warnock and Lori Henderson

Published by Familius LLC, www.familius.com

Familius books are available at special discounts for bulk purchases, whether for sales promotions or for family or corporate use. For more information, contact Familius Sales at 559-876-2170 or email orders@familius.com.

Library of Congress Cataloging-in-Publication Data
2016942208

Print ISBN 9781942934691
Ebook ISBN 9781944822163

Printed in the United States of America

Edited by Emily Faison
Cover design by David Miles
Book design by David Miles and Kurt Wahlner

10 9 8 7 6 5 4 3 2 1

First Edition

CONTENTS

WHAT IS
A MiNDfUL MEAL?

I recently made a pot of soup. I often make soup, but this soup was different. Not because the ingredients were unique but because I was engaged in the preparation. The recipe instructed me to mince the onion, slice the carrots, dice the squash, chop the asparagus, and grate the zucchini into "noodles." I found myself enjoying each step and appreciating the colors, textures, aromas, and flavors of each vegetable. I felt the pleasure of having grown some of them in my garden.

I pondered the path of the others involved: the farmers, who cared enough to plant organic seeds and grow the vegetables in a healthy and earth-sustainable manner; the soil, pulsing with life and life-giving minerals; the water, which enabled the little seeds to grow to maturity; the sun, generously warming the soil and sharing its light for the plants to grow and for us to witness the miracle of plant life; the honeybees, drawn by the colors and scents of each tiny blossom to pollinate and awaken the vegetables to life. Pondering all the potential inherent in each tiny seed is exhilarating!

I put all the vegetables together in a pot of broth (vegetarian, in this case) and let them blend to perfection. Infused with the energies of joy and gratitude, I knew this would be a happy, healthy meal.

While the soup simmered and filled the kitchen with lovely aromas, I prepared the salad with the same mindfulness as I had prepared the soup: a beautiful mix of fresh greens of varying shades and textures, topped with a fan of pear slices, chopped walnuts, a sprinkling of dried cranberries, and a drizzle of homemade salad dressing. The final adornment: a trio of red, orange, and yellow nasturtium flowers, edible, with a mild radish flavor.

Now it was time to set the table. I set out some pretty plates and bowls and thought tenderly of my sister, who had recently passed away. These dishes had belonged to her, and she offered them to me shortly before her passing. I filled the glasses with purified water—something I am grateful to have access to. I put out a plate of natural yeast sourdough bread with homemade butter, then I hurried to my herb garden and filled a vase with flowering peppermint and lavender stems. The bees were buzzing on the tiny blossoms—music to my ears.

As I completed all the preparations, I thought about a new friend who would arrive shortly to share this modest meal. What would we talk about? What would we have in common? Would she appreciate and value the same things—organic, healthful foods; nature's gifts; simple beauty; pretty dishes?

Indeed. As we sat, she asked if she could offer a blessing on the food. She expressed gratitude for the colors and beauty and healthfulness of the foods we were about to eat and for the blessing of friendship. As we eagerly feasted, she asked: "Have you ever practiced mindfulness?"

I felt my heart smile!

> **FRIENDSHIP IS BORN AT THAT MOMENT WHEN ONE PERSON SAYS TO ANOTHER: "WHAT! YOU TOO? I THOUGHT I WAS THE ONLY ONE."**
> **—C. S. LEWIS**

A MINDFUL KITCHEN

Learning to choose wholesome, healthy foods over man-made pseudofoods is a journey. In classes and on my radio show, I teach my students to celebrate friendship, etiquette, taste, texture, aroma, and beauty and the sound of joyful conversation, music, laughter, expressions of gratitude, and gladness.

Several years ago, I attended a lecture by Michael Pollan at Abravanel Hall in Salt Lake City, Utah. Slow Food Utah organizers had invited him to speak about the nature of food, our environment, and healthful eating. He displayed on a large screen a photo of a decadently rich and luscious slice of chocolate cake. The reaction, as he expected, was a collective groan of desire and guilt from the audience. In America, he explained, that is the general reaction. But he encouraged us to think about food in a new way. In France, he explained, the reaction to a slice of cake is one of celebration, not guilt.

One of my favorite books is *French Women Don't Get Fat: The Secret of Eating for Pleasure* by Mireille Guiliano, an absolutely delightful and inspiring read. It seems that French people seem to live with wisdom, taking pleasure in staying thin by eating well, while Americans typically see food as a conflict and obsess over it. The French think about good things to eat, while Americans worry about what might be bad for us. The French don't eat "fat-free," "sugar-free," or anything artificially stripped of natural flavor. They go for the real thing in moderation. They eat with all five senses, allowing less to seem like more. They care enormously about the presentation of food, and they don't diet.

As we ponder our relationship with the earth and food, a

new perspective takes shape. New gratitude flows from deep within as we learn to experience what good food offers us. I believe in a loving God who has given us the earth to be used with wisdom and judgment. People focused on doing good in the world are rewarded with the good things of the earth, the fullness of the earth—herbs, orchards, and gardens in season, created for the benefit and the use of humankind, to please the eye and to gladden the heart, to strengthen the body and to enliven the soul.

As I have learned more about authentic, mindful food and its connection to happiness, I have made a personal commitment to a wholesome diet. I drink purified water, the beverage of choice in my home most of the time. I generally have a green smoothie every day, made with living greens and fruits in season, preferably from my garden. I choose to eat organic whenever possible. The bulk of my family's daily diet is healthful fruits and vegetables, mostly raw. In the colder months, we grow greens on our kitchen counter (herbs, sprouts, and microgreens) and with cold frames over our garden boxes. Raw nuts and seeds are a daily staple, usually soaked and sprouted for superior nutrition. Legumes are a staple and are usually not from a can—soaked and slow cooked is best. Grains are limited and usually sprouted and cooked over low heat for cereals. We grind our own fresh whole-grain flours, roll our own oats, and very rarely use white flour. If I choose to use white flour, it must be unbleached and unbromated.

At our house, we choose to eat meat only during the coldest winter months, from animals humanely raised, free range, and processed at local farms that we have visited. (May I add: these animals and their farmers are happy!) We make our own butter, kefir, and yogurt from raw milk and buy cream from a local dairy farmer. We use no artificial or refined sugars. When called for, we sweeten with natural sweeteners in their whole raw forms that contain nutrients, including dates, organic coconut palm sugar, home-grown stevia leaves, local raw honey, organic pure maple syrup, evaporated cane juice crystals, agave, and xylitol. I do not eat "in fear" of healthy fats. Instead, 70% of our daily caloric intake should come from healthy fats, including avocados, coconut oil, cold-pressed extra virgin olive oil, flax oil, hemp seed oil, nuts, and seeds.

There are also things we mindfully avoid. We choose to forego vegetable oils, which are highly processed and grown using genetic modification. We don't drink soda or consume anything with high fructose corn syrup, aspartame and other artificial sweeteners, artificial colors and flavorings, chemical and synthetic additives, MSG, trans fats, preservatives, pro-cessed foods, or meat or milk raised in concentrated animal feeding operations (CAFOs) and treated with antibiotics and growth hormones.

We can, with gratitude and without remorse, indulge in beautiful, festive, and delicious celebrations of tasty foods that tickle our palates and delight our spirits.

IS IT MINDFUL?

Creating a mindful life is simple, and doesn't need to be over-thought. It's all about taking responsibility for thinking about three things before you eat:

1   Is my food naturally good for me?

2   Am I eating a healthy balance of nutrients each day?

3   Do I stop when I've eaten enough?

Below are some simple guidelines for creating a mindful table, but remember, your definition of mindfulness is ultimately your responsibility. The core of mindfulness is taking responsibility for your own life and choices. Good decisions are usually the product of thought and discussion. Test your logic by making sure you can explain the reasons for your food choices in simple terms, using reliable, vetted information from specific sources. Finally, encourage your friends and family to question your decisions so you can explore and examine your own logic.

With that in mind, ask yourself: Is it mindful to eat . . .

Microwave-cooked food?

Up to you.

Lori doesn't. I do sparingly. Read primary scientific studies. Be mindful of the pitfalls of Internet rumors and opinions, which are much easier to find than science-based facts.

Frozen food?

Yes.

Why? Because freezing is a great way to preserve food without chemicals or additives. Natural frozen ingredients of a huge variety are easily available to families and often more affordable.

Canned food?

Up to you.

Be mindful of additives, preservatives, and the issue of potentially harmful plastic linings in metal cans. Be aware that many fruits in cans are packed with sugar-added syrups. These syrups should be drained, not eaten, to avoid the extra sugar. Even canned soups often have added sugars.

Genetically modified foods?

Probably not.

You can make up your own mind about whether the world's food supply should be natural or genetically manipulated, but keep this in mind: Why does it need to be genetically modified? Who stands to benefit financially when food is genetically modified? Vote with your money. Buy only the kind of food you want to support, and buy only from companies that provide the information you want. If a company will not clearly tell you everything you want to know about the origin of your food, don't buy from them.

Fresh food?

Of course!

But consider this: how local is your fresh food? Consider growing your own in a garden, small or large. If you don't want to garden, look for local food sold by local growers at farmer's markets. Probably the last resort should be fresh food shipped hundreds of miles. Remember that the number one reason for genetically modifying food is to prevent foods from naturally spoiling. Foods shipped over long distances and stored for weeks and months tend to be genetically modified, including fruits, melons, and vegetables.

Meat?

Up to you.

If you do choose to eat meat, remember to eat more vegetables, grains, and fruits than meat by volume in every meal for the best healthy balance.

White flour?

Up to you.

If you are still eating white flour, the concept of mindfulness would ask you to read up about how white flour, white rice, and other starches spike the glycemic index just like sugar and are most void of the fiber and nutrients necessary for a healthy life. Whole grains are what the body needs.

Raw or cooked food?

Both.

Raw food has advantages, as does cooked food. We need to have both on our plates daily for our best health.

Sugar? Sweeteners? Treats?

In moderation.

We all want sweets in our lives. But mindfulness says we are careful and we eat only natural foods in modest amounts.

Fad diets? Celebrity diets? Austerity diets?

No. Never.

Why? Because no one else has responsibility for your food choices. You know and we know that fad diets end up hurting more than they help. The only kind of "diet" that is really helpful is the diet that can be sustained for a lifetime, not thirty days.

With shame?
Because of addiction?
With heartache?

No.

If you find yourself eating in a way that is not mindful, just stop. Start your mindful plan over again. Don't waste even a minute shaming yourself or listing excuses or hating yourself.

Mindfulness means that you don't waste time on nonsense. We all make some decisions that could have been better. What is important is being honest with ourselves. Simply stop doing what you shouldn't be doing and start anew. And if you get off track, stop it and start anew again. No matter how often you need to start anew, just do it. Don't waste time shaming yourself for past decisions, even if that past decision was five minutes ago. Always look forward. Your only job as a human being is to be a better person today than you were yesterday. This is the core of the mindful life.

MINDFULNESS: CHEWING

We are made to chew. Using our teeth is part of the joy of dining. Chewing stimulates our digestive tract and colon, and chewing stimulates the body's production of digestive enzymes, so we need to embrace chewing for good health. Here are simple suggestions toward embracing mindful chewing:

- **Start each meal with a simple raw salad.** This could be a traditional lettuce salad with dressing and your favorite salad additions—I am partial to hard-boiled eggs, peas, cucumbers, and chickpeas with croutons over romaine, topped with shredded cheese, sunflower seeds, and other seeds.

- **Crunch on vegetables—the more unusual and flavorful, the better.** I am partial to sticks of peeled non-bleeding types of beets—chioggia, golden, or albino sugar beets—golden turnips, or carrots in myriad colors. Color brightens the plate and brings joy to the flavor. It is not always necessary to have a full plate of assorted raw vegetables for you and your family to choose from. Sometimes, one simple, quick-peeled fresh raw beet or carrot is the best choice. And you don't have to limit yourself to baby carrots. When you feel adventurous, try these raw: kohlrabi, parsnips, celeriac, rutabaga, red celery, sweet squash, turnips, maca, sunchokes, parsley root. (There are numerous fruits to try, as well, such as pomelo, persimmons, Asian pears, litchi, and more.)

- **Make nuts a regular part of your eating experience.** If you have a smoothie for breakfast, eat a handful of cashews, almonds, peanuts, or pecans with the smoothie.

- **Try adding whole grain toast to your meal.** Whole grain toast is a simple, quick way to get your teeth into an appetizer. And feel free to butter up your toast, because wholesome, natural fats, in moderation, are part of a mindful diet.

THE MINDFUL EMBRACE OF BUTTER, OIL, AND NATURAL FATS

Don't be afraid of fats! The low-fat, no-fat craze from the 1970s has done a lot of damage. Our brain is 70% fat, and we need to feed ourselves healthy fats to function properly. Healthy oils can be added to some foods without being heated, which is the best way for the body to take full advantage of the oil's nutrients.

At some point in the American psyche, butter became the enemy. Millions of dollars were spent on advertising campaigns to convince the public to purchase butter substitutes claiming to be better than all-natural butter. Today, most health enthusiasts consider the national margarine experiment to have been a failure, and food lovers everywhere are mindfully embracing natural healthy fats like butter, cream, olive oil, and coconut oil, in part because fat substitutes may be made with trans fats and chemicals.

"In recent years, a number of studies have cast doubt on the health benefits of the traditional low-fat diet," reported the *New York Times* in a 2015 article titled "Consumers Are Embracing Full-Fat Foods."[1] The article reported that sales of butter in the United States jumped 14% in 2014 and another 6% in the first three months of 2015. Sales of whole milk rose 11% in the first half of 2015; skim milk sales fell 14%. Experts predicted a spike in purchases of red meat and eggs in the coming years.

In a 2014 op-ed for the *New York Times*, venerable food writer Mark Bittman pronounced that butter is back. "Julia Child, goddess of fat, is beaming somewhere," he said, echoing something I

THE WHOLE POINT OF BEING MINDFUL IS TO ENJOY BEING ALIVE

have said for years. When asked about why I refused to cook with margarine or any butter substitute, I have often said, "No one ate more butter than Julia Child, and she lived to be ninety-one years old!"[2]

Why not mindfully embrace the flavor of butter—a genuinely natural and historic food—in moderation? The whole point of being mindful is to enjoy being alive by embracing the pleasures of food with the responsibility of personal healthy limits.

Butter has more to offer than just flavor. Butter contains 7% of your daily recommended value of vitamin A and 2% of your vitamin D, according to USDA data. The health benefits of coconut oil and olive oil are now universally recognized—and even lard has come back into vogue for its health benefits. As we are bombarded with commercials for pharmaceutical drugs, are hocked processed powders and supplements, and hear more about the dubious origins and outright scams involving supplements that, when tested by government agencies, don't even contain the ingredients listed on the packaging, is it any wonder that the public has developed a new desire to embrace genuine, true food as the primary source of health and nutrition?

ZEN OF THE KNIFE

A critical part of mindful eating is "leaning in" to the experience of home food preparation. I was once teaching a class at my home, allowing students to sample various fresh vegetables from my garden, when a student asked what gadget I used to prepare all these vegetables for the family table. To the astonishment and angst of the student, I showed the class my favorite knife. She was amazed and felt a bit betrayed—was there no gadget, no miracle machine, no fancy electric appliance? No. As any chef can tell you, the knife is the pen for the poet in the kitchen. This student made it clear to me and the whole class that she considered the work of peeling and slicing vegetables to be drudgery and boredom—a punishment and a chore.

This person may never find health—or joy—in the kitchen.

The kitchen cannot be a prison. When we find no joy in cooking, a home becomes a food desert. Soda, packaged products, processed foods, and frozen meals reign. Fresh, real food—the kind that is chopped, sliced, peeled, diced, minced, and julienned—is shunted aside for so-called convenience.

Freedom is found in simplicity. What is really needed in the kitchen is colorful vegetables and fruits, fresh and raw, a knife, and good quality meats, if you choose to eat meat. (I do; Lori does not.) There is authentic magic in making simple, quick cheeses at home, in cutting carrots, spiraling squash, and slicing beets. Accomplished home cooks know that preparing fruits and vegetables takes only minutes and can be relaxing, pleasurable, and even therapeutic. And the highest order of pleasure in the kitchen comes from preparing a simple, quick, and supremely healthy meal using ingredients from your own garden. The feeling of love and confidence that comes from living and eating in this way cannot be matched by buying a frozen meal in a big box store or touched by driving your car through a fast-food lane. Some days, we might need to turn to a frozen meal, carefully chosen, or a quick-food restaurant. Our lives are not perfect. We do good, then better, and we work to become our best selves inside the kitchen and out.

WASTE LESS
WITH LESS WAIST

Author Melissa Richardson once told a group of people that the key to preparing family meals is to think two meals ahead. I have begun to believe this might be the entire key to success in the kitchen. We try to create menus from what is in season and is fresh and ready and calling out to us in our garden. Planning two meals ahead gives the home cook power. We can be prepared instead of panicked. We can match our preparation time to our schedule. We can better use what we have in the fridge and garden. We waste less with less waist, if you will: as we are mindful in our choices about what we put in our mouth, we weigh less, too.

In real life, planning ahead is not always possible. It is important to acknowledge this up front because we have to be prepared to "reset" our choices when life does not go our way. When we lose control, we can be quick to "repent" by stepping back and starting again. But every home cook is better prepared with an arsenal of quick, simple, healthy meals that can be made in minutes with mindful ingredients. That is what this book is all about.

ENDNOTES

1. Anahad O'Connor, "Consumers Are Embracing Full-Fat Foods," *New York Times*, September 23, 2015, http://well.blogs.nytimes.com/2015/09/23/consumers-are-embracing-full-fat-foods/?_r=0.

2. Mark Bittman, "Butter Is Back," *New York Times*, March 25, 2014, http://www.nytimes.com/2014/03/26/opinion/bittman-butter-is-back.html.

BREAKFAST

SIMPLE SMOOTHIES

For best results, use a high-speed blender. The yield is about 5 cups. This can be doubled to split between two days. It's a ready breakfast for the next day!

2 cups liquid:

- Purified water
- Water kefir
- Real coconut water (no added sweeteners)
- 1 cup water + 1 cup juice (We don't recommend juice, because it's basically sugar water and therefore not mindful eating.)

2 handfuls of leafy greens

- Use a combination of two or three types of greens.
- Spinach is always a good base because it is mild and

helps to mellow other stronger ones like kale, collards, beet greens, etc.

- If you use parsley, use a small amount. Too much will make your smoothie bitter.

2 veggies

- Cucumber
- Celery
- Carrot
- Beet
- Zucchini
- Broccoli and cauliflower (experiment with anything you have)

2 fruits

- Half or whole: banana, apple, pear, pineapple chunks, persimmon, or peaches
- Slice of lemon or lime with rind or fresh ginger
- 2–3 pitted dates
- Berries of all kinds
- Frozen fruit*

2 tablespoons of any of the following healthy fats or a combination:

- Half an avocado
  (Produces a deliciously creamy smoothie!)
- Coconut oil
- Olive oil
- Almond oil
- Flax oil
- Nuts
- Seeds: sesame, sunflower, chia, psyllium, hemp, flax**

*Frozen fruit produces a delightfully frosty smoothie. Consider your needs: note that freezing kills the enzymes that make it a living food.

**Chia, psyllium, hemp, and flax have omega-3 fatty acids and assist in bowel elimination.

OPTIONAL SMOOTHIE INGREDIENTS:

- Natural yeast, which is both prebiotic and probiotic. You could add 2 tablespoons of natural yeast (which is not store-bought yeast; see SeedRenaissance.com for details).
- You can add anything you have in your garden or fridge. When using herbs with a strong flavor, use small amounts.

- cilantro (adds flavor and nutrients)
- parsley (adds flavor and nutrients)
- tarragon (adds a bit of protein, as well as flavor and nutrients)
- sage (adds flavor and nutrients)
- garlic chives (adds flavor and nutrients)
- oregano (adds flavor and nutrients)
- marjoram (adds flavor and nutrients)
- protein powder (adds protein)
- yogurt (great for calcium, probiotic bacteria, and enzymes; also adds creaminess)
- coconut milk (adds sweetness)
- cucumber (adds flavor and nutrients)
- mango (adds color, flavor, and nutrients)
- sprouts: peas, sunflower, alfalfa, clover (adds flavor and nutrients)
- spinach (helps mellow other flavors and adds nutrients)
- kale (nutritional powerhouse)
- collard (nutritional powerhouse)
- beet greens (adds flavor and nutrients)
- mustard greens (adds a touch of heat, flavor, and nutrients)
- bananas (adds sweetness and creaminess)
- avocado (adds protein and creaminess)

- cashews (adds protein and creaminess)
- broccoli (adds flavor and nutrients)
- brussels sprouts (adds flavor and nutrients)
- cauliflower (adds flavor and nutrients)
- pineapple (powerhouse of nutrients; also adds sweetness)
- brown banana peels (Lori's husband, Matt, adds these. He says, "You can't taste it, and there are health benefits.")
- lemons with peel (adds flavor and nutrients)
- fresh ginger (adds flavor and nutrients)
- essential oils: lemon, peppermint, ginger—just a drop (adds flavor and aids in digestion)
- frozen berries (adds color, sweetness, flavor, and nutrients)
- apples and pears (adds sweetness, flavor, and nutrients)
- flaxseed oil (adds protein, nutrients, fiber, and omega-3 fatty acids)
- psyllium (adds fiber)
- chia seeds (adds protein, fiber, and omega-3 fatty acids)
- milk kefir (adds protein, probiotics, and creaminess)
- stevia (adds sweetness without calories)
- pumpkin puree (adds flavor and nutrients)
- peaches (adds flavor and nutrients)

- ○ oatmeal (adds fiber, protein, and nutrients)
- ○ coconut palm sugar (in small amounts, adds nutrients)
- ○ dates—pitted (adds sweetness and flavor)

MAKE-AHEAD BREAKFAST

Pancakes, waffles, and crepes are easy to make in large batches and easy to freeze in baggies for individual servings on a busy morning.

TOPPINGS:

- Spread a whole grain pancake or crepe with a nut butter and sliced bananas and roll up for an on-the-go breakfast or an after-school snack.
- Top waffles with fresh berries, applesauce, or peaches.
- Fruit syrup: Lori makes a 30-second fruit syrup with a can of fruit, like bottled peaches. Pour off some of the liquid and blend. Add a little cinnamon and a sprinkling of sugar if desired.

LUNCH

HOT SANDWICHES

Serve with raw, crisp vegetables on the side.

CRAVING TURKEY CRANBERRY SANDWICHES

Adapted from one of my favorite restaurants, Cravings. This is a perfect hot sandwich for a cold winter day!

1. Butter a slice of your favorite bread and put it on medium low heat in a frying pan. Mix a tablespoon of cranberry sauce with a tablespoon of mayonnaise and put half of this on the face of the bread.

2. Add a slice of swiss cheese, two slices of oven-roasted deli turkey, a layer of thinly sliced sweet apples (or tart, if you prefer), and a half slice of swiss cheese.

3. Butter another slice of bread, put the remaining cran-

berry mayonnaise on the other side, and place it mayonnaise-down on the sandwich cooking in the skillet. As soon as the bottom is brown, flip the sandwich. Serve warm.

ROSEMARY TURKEY SANDWICHES

A savory variation of the Craving sandwich.

1. Butter a slice of rosemary focaccia or other rosemary artisan bread and put it on medium-low heat in a frying pan.

2. Add a slice of Swiss cheese and sprinkle lightly with fresh or dried rosemary.

3. Add two slices of oven-roasted deli turkey, a layer of thinly sliced tart apples, and a half slice of swiss cheese.

4. Butter another slice of bread and place it down on the sandwich cooking in the skillet. As soon as the bottom is brown, flip the sandwich. Serve warm.

APPLE BACON CHEDDAR MELT

1. Brown red or yellow onions in butter in a frying pan for about five minutes.

2. Butter a slice of your favorite bread and put it on medium low heat in a frying pan. Spread with mayonnaise and add softened onions.

3. Add a slice of medium or sharp cheddar cheese, 2–3 slices of cooked bacon, a layer of thinly sliced tart green apples, and a half slice of cheddar cheese (you don't want too much cheese).

4. Butter another slice of bread, put mayonnaise on the other side, and place it mayonnaise-down on the sandwich cooking in the skillet. As soon as the bottom is brown, flip the sandwich. Serve immediately.

GRILLED CHEESE VARIATIONS

- Start with artisan or sandwich bread such as cinnamon raisin, asiago, garlic, whole wheat, or multigrain.

- Add artisan or sliced cheeses like creamy havarti or other havarti varieties, sharp cheddar, provolone, or gorgonzola.

- Add deli meats or pulled meats, like smoked sausage or salami.

- For spreads, try cranberry or other sweet mayonnaise, jalapeño or other spicy jelly, herb mayonnaise, or vegan butter.

- Add sliced fruit to cook inside the sandwich: tart apple, sweet apple, persimmon, Asian pear, mango, or papaya.

HAVARTI BACON SANDWICHES

1 Butter a slice of your favorite bread and put it on medium-low heat in a frying pan.

2 Add a slice of havarti cheese, two slices of cooked bacon, a layer of thinly sliced sweet apples, and another slice of havarti.

3   Butter another slice of bread and place it on the sandwich. As soon as the bottom is brown, flip the sandwich. Serve warm.

HAM & EGG SANDWICHES

1   Fry a slice of deli ham and an egg separately in a pan.

2   Remove the ham and egg from the pan, then toast two slices of buttered bread in the pan.

3   Combine to make a sandwich and serve warm.

NAAN SANDWICHES

1   Sauté chicken with colorful sweet peppers, onion, garlic, and a splash of water.

2   Top with feta and serve on a pita or naan.

3   Top with a fried egg and salsa. Serve with steamed vegetables on the side.

CLASSIC MELT

1. Using swiss cheese (or sharp cheddar or havarti) and fresh tomato slices over a tuna sandwich, cook in a toaster oven until cheese melts.

   TIP: TRY CANNED HAM INSTEAD OF TUNA.

CRISPY CHEESE TACO SANDWICHES

1. Put one slice of your favorite taco cheese (or 1 heaping tablespoon shredded cheese) in the center of a frying pan over medium-low heat.

2. Once the cheese begins to melt, sprinkle roughly 1/4 cup prepared taco meat over the cheese.

3. Cook until the cheese begins to brown on the bottom (3–4 minutes) and then remove to a piece of toasted bread to eat.

POCKET SANDWICHES

Shredded vegetables cook faster than vegetables in chunks, and for the sake of speed, this recipe uses shredded vegetables: any blend of broccoli, kale, spinach, chard stalks, carrots, onion, or other vegetables.

1. Boil the shredded vegetable of your choice in 1/4 cup water until the water dissipates, then add a dab of butter to the pan, add an egg, and scramble.

2. Add cubed ham, shredded chicken, pepperoni, or other meat as desired. Serve in half a pita, warmed.

SCOTCH EGG SANDWICH

Traditional baked Scotch eggs are not possible to make in 15 minutes, but there is a way to "hack" the traditional recipe.

1. Cook breakfast sausage in a frying pan.

2. When the sausage is mostly cooked, drain the fat and scramble one egg per sandwich in the pan with the sausage.

3. Serve open-face on toast. Swiss cheese can be added if desired.

COLD SANDWICHES

Serve with raw or steamed vegetables on the side.

HAM SALAD SANDWICHES

1. Toss together cubed fully cooked ham (or canned ham), chopped hard-boiled eggs, chopped celery or chard stalk, pickle relish, mayonnaise, yellow mustard, and chopped onion.

2. Serve on your favorite sandwich bread.

NO-BREAD APPLE SANDWICHES

1. Make whole apple slices by cutting slices from either side of the core of the whole apple (or remove the core and slice the apple horizontally, for slices with holes in the center).

2. Spread your favorite nut butter (peanut, cashew, almond) over a slice and drizzle slightly with honey.

3. Sprinkle with your favorite granola (optional) and top with another apple slice.

TIP: YOU CAN ALSO TRY SPRINKLING WITH CHOCO-LATE CHIPS, CAROB CHUNKS, CHOPPED DATES, OR ANY DRIED FRUIT INSTEAD OF HONEY.

BLT APPLE SANDWICH

1 Make whole apple slices by cutting slices from either side of the core of the whole apple (or remove the core and slice the apple horizontally, for slices with holes in the center).

2 Add cooked bacon, crisp lettuce, fresh tomato slices, and a slice of swiss, havarti, or sharp cheddar cheese for a quick summer sandwich.

LUNCH CONDIMENTS

FAST FRESH PESTO

- 1/3 cup minced fresh basil
- 1/4 cup minced fresh parsley
- 1/4 cup grated parmesan cheese
- 1/2 teaspoon salt (optional)
- 1 garlic clove, quartered
- 1/8 teaspoon freshly ground nutmeg
- 1/4–1/3 cup olive oil

1 In a blender or food processor, combine all ingredients except olive oil. Cover and process on low for 1 minute or until very finely chopped. While processing, gradually add olive oil in a steady stream until the mixture reaches your desired consistency.

2   Use for pasta and vegetables; mix with homemade mayonnaise (below) for a delicious spread on veggie or meat sandwiches!

TIP: FREEZE PESTO IN ICE CUBE TRAYS FOR QUICK SIN-GLE SERVINGS!

DELICIOUS 30-SECOND HOMEMADE MAYONNAISE

- 1 cup sunflower or safflower oil
- 1 large egg
- 1 teaspoon fresh lemon juice
- 1 teaspoon raw apple cider vinegar
- 1 teaspoon dry mustard
- 1/2 teaspoon salt
- Pinch of white or black ground pepper (optional)

1   Fully incorporate all ingredients in a blender or with a stick blender for about 30 seconds.

2   Serve chilled. Keep refrigerated; use within one week.

HOMEMADE TACO SEASONING

- 1 tablespoon chili powder
- 1/2 teaspoon garlic powder
- 1/4 teaspoon onion powder
- 1/2 teaspoon dried oregano, marjoram, or Italian seasoning
- 1/2 teaspoon paprika
- 1 1/2 teaspoons ground cumin
- 1 teaspoon salt
- 1 teaspoon black pepper
- 1 teaspoon dried sweet mace, summer savory, or winter savory
- 1 teaspoon turmeric

1   Combine all ingredients. Store in a lidded, airtight container in a cupboard or in the fridge.

2   Add 1/2 cup water and 2 teaspoons (or more, to taste) of seasoning per pound of cooked and drained ground beef. You can also use the above recipe in cups instead of teaspoons to make and store in bulk.

HOT SOUPS

Serve with a side salad or bread.

TACO SOUP

- 1 onion, diced
- 1/2 pound ground beef
- 1 can red or black beans
- 1 can corn
- 2 fresh tomatoes, diced, 1 can diced tomatoes, or 1 can tomato paste
- 1 teaspoon chili powder or taco seasoning

1   Sauté the onions in a stew pot until soft.

2   Add ground beef; brown and drain.

3   Add all remaining ingredients and bring to a boil. Serve with your favorite tortilla chips.

LENTIL "ADD IN" SOUP

- 1 cup steamed or grilled carrots
- 2 cups kale, chopped
- 1/2 cup green peppers, chopped
- 2–3 green onions, chopped
- 1 can yams or 1 whole yam
- 1 can organic lentil soup

1. Season veggies to taste with small amounts of garlic powder, curry, chili powder, butter, salt, and pepper.

2. Dump veggies in the soup with drippings. Optional: serve over rice.

LORI'S ITALIAN WINTER SOUP

- 1 quart chicken broth
- 2 potatoes with skins, sliced and quartered
- 3 cups chopped kale
- 1/2 pound Italian sausage (optional)
- 1/4 teaspoon salt
- 1/4 teaspoon crushed red pepper flakes
- 1 jalapeño (optional)

1. Combine all ingredients and simmer.

HEARTY VEGETABLE SOUP

A great option if you aren't feeling well. The hot peppers help to clear the sinuses, and the soup may help boost your immune system when sick!

1. Combine and simmer tomato juice, broth, shredded cabbage, celery, carrots, onion, and garlic.

2. Add optional meat (choose broth to complement meat).

3. Add herbs like parsley, oregano, thyme, tarragon, etc.

4. Add salt, freshly ground black pepper, and jalapeno peppers.

5. Add canned green beans, sliced zucchini, and mushrooms during last 10 minutes of simmering.

WHITE BEAN & GREENS STEW

- 1/2 pound sausage
- 1 can white beans
- 2 fresh tomatoes, diced, or 1 can diced tomatoes
- 1 handful greens

1   Add all ingredients except greens to a soup pot and heat to boiling.

2   Add greens and stir until wilted. Serve immediately.

MEATBALL SOUP

- 1 package fresh or frozen tortellini
- 1 pound prepared meatballs
- 1 can spaghetti sauce
- 1 handful spinach or greens

1   Add all ingredients except greens to a soup pot and heat to boiling.

2   Add greens and stir until wilted. Serve immediately.

CAULIFLOWER CORIANDER SOUP

- 3 tablespoons olive or coconut oil
- 1 onion, chopped
- 4 garlic cloves
- 1 1-inch piece of fresh ginger, peeled
- 1 teaspoon cumin
- 2 teaspoons coriander
- 1/4 teaspoon turmeric
- 1/8 teaspoon cayenne pepper
- 2 potatoes
- 2 cups cauliflower florets
- 7 cups chicken stock
- 1 cup cream

1. In a frying pan, heat the oil and add the onion, garlic, and ginger. Stir and cook until onions are softened—about 4 minutes.

2. Add spices and stir 1 minute.

3. Add potatoes, cauliflower, and stock. Bring to a boil and simmer until the potatoes are tender—about 10 minutes.

4. Salt to taste. Add cream and serve hot.

APPLE SOUP

 Simmer together low-sodium chicken or vegetable broth, carrots, apples, fresh ginger, and curry powder.

COCONUT CHICKEN SOUP

- 1 onion, chopped
- 1 tablespoon coconut oil
- 1 quart chicken broth
- 1 1/2 cups shredded carrots
- 1 pound shredded cooked chicken
- 14 ounces coconut water
- 2 cloves garlic, chopped
- 1 1/4-inch cube of fresh ginger, chopped
- 1/2 tablespoon chili powder
- 2 cups chopped spinach, chard leaves, beet greens, or other fresh greens
- 1/2 cup chopped cilantro
- Juice of 2 limes
- 1 cup chopped green onions (optional)
- Salt and pepper to taste

1. In a soup pan over medium heat, soften the chopped onion in the coconut oil.

2. Add broth and carrots and simmer until the carrots are tender, about 5 minutes.

3. Add remaining ingredients and simmer 2 minutes. Serve warm.

LORI'S CLASSIC POTATO LEEK SOUP

- 3 potatoes, cut into cubes
- 3 cups cleaned chopped leeks
- 1 stalk celery, sliced
- 1 carrot, sliced
- 4 tablespoons butter
- 3/4 teaspoon salt
- 1/2 cup chicken stock
- 1 onion, minced (optional)
- Dash of nutmeg (optional)
- 1 clove minced garlic (optional)
- Dash of thyme, marjoram, or basil (optional)
- 3 cups cold milk

1. Bring all ingredients except milk to a boil until vegetables are tender.

2. Remove from heat. Stir in milk.

3. Blend soup in a blender until smooth. Serve hot.

CHILLED SOUPS

LORI'S PUMPKIN BLENDER SOUP

- 2 cups carrot juice
- 1 small can pumpkin puree
- 1 teaspoon pumpkin pie spice
- 1 avocado, diced
- 4 dates, pitted

1. Combine ingredients in blender and blend until smooth and creamy.

2. Adjust ingredients to desired consistency. Serve hot or cold.

TIP: TRY ADDING SAUTÉED ONIONS AND/OR LEEKS.

WATERMELON SOUP

- 1 small or medium watermelon, or 1 honeydew melon
- 1 mango
- 1 lime
- 1 cup sparkling grape juice
- 1/2 cucumber
- 1/4 cube fresh ginger

1. Trim and cube the fruit.

2. Add all ingredients to a blender or food processor and pulse until smooth. Chill or add several ice cubes and pulse again until smooth. Serve immediately.

STRAWBERRY BALSAMIC SOUP

- 5 cups strawberries, stems removed
- 2 cups half-and-half
- 1 1/4 cups sour cream
- 1/4 cup honey
- 1/4 cup balsamic vinegar

1. Add all ingredients to a blender, blend until smooth, and serve chilled.

PEACH SOUP

- 1 quart plain yogurt
- Peaches, to taste
- 2–3 drops almond extract

1   Blend all ingredients and serve chilled.

ASPARAGUS SOUP

- 8 ounces asparagus, fresh or frozen
- 1 onion, chopped
- 1/2 cup boiling water
- 1 cup milk
- 1/2 cup half-and-half
- 1/2 teaspoon salt
- Dash of pepper

1   Cook the vegetables in the boiling water until just tender.

2   Remove from heat and cool for a few minutes. Do not drain. Instead, pour vegetables and water into a blender.

3 Add remaining ingredients and blend until smooth.
Serve warm or chilled.

TIP: THIS SOUP CAN ALSO BE MADE WITH PEAS OR ANY
GARDEN GREENS IN SUBSTITUTION FOR ASPARAGUS.

SALADS

SALAD COMPONENTS

Greens

- Spinach
- Romaine
- Celery hearts, celery slices, or celery leaves
- Dandelion leaves
- Gourmet lettuces
- Mustard greens
- Asian greens
- Beet greens
- Baby turnip greens
- Cold frame greens in winter
- Herbs
- Microgreens and sprouts (You can grow these on your own kitchen counter!)

Proteins

- Smoked trout
- Shrimp
- Cubed ham
- Pulled pork (sweet or barbecue)
- Diced turkey
- Shredded chicken
- Feta, cheddar cubes, parmesan cubes or parmesan shaved with vegetable peeler, or your favorite cheese
- Tuna
- Taco meat
- Pecans, walnuts, almond slivers, toasted pine nuts, pepitas (pumpkin or squash seeds), sunflower seeds, or sesame seeds (these can be used lightly toasted, raw, or roasted from the store)
- Sweetened nuts

MAKE YOUR OWN SWEETENED NUTS

Pecans, almonds, and walnuts add a delicious elegance to any salad when lightly sweetened. To sweeten, heat a tablespoon of sugar in frying pan, add nuts, and stir continually until sugar liquefies and coats nuts. Spread on parchment to cool. Break apart and sprinkle on salad just before serving.

SALAD BLEND IDEAS

- **Citrus salad:** grapefruit, pomelo, orange, blood orange, mandarin, or tangerine
- **Grain and seed salad:** quinoa, orach, flax, chia, amaranth, or pumpkin seeds
- **Melon salad:** honeydew, cantaloupe, watermelon, or citron
- **Greek salad:** chopped broccoli, red onion, olives (kalamata are best, but black olives work, too), cucumber, bell pepper, and tomato; feta cheese crumbles; vinaigrette of balsamic vinegar, lemon juice, olive oil, and oregano

- **Classic chopped salad:** 1/4 cup lemon juice, extra-virgin olive oil, garlic, salt, pepper, romaine, tomatoes, olives, 2 cans drained tuna
- **Brook salad:** avocado, tomato, black beans, corn, cilantro, lime juice, romaine lettuce, purple/red onion
- **Classic caprese salad:** basil leaves topped with fresh mozzarella slices and tomato slices, drizzled with olive oil and a touch of salt and pepper.
- **Taco salad:** taco meat, prepared beans, cubed tomatoes, ranch dressing, and shredded lettuce, served in a taco shell bowl or over tortilla chips.
- **Chicken or turkey salad:** cooked chicken or turkey over salad with water chestnuts, cashews, green onion, celery, grapes, pineapple tidbits, and homemade mayonnaise (see recipe on page 41).
- **Spinach salad:** spinach with mushrooms, green onions, bacon, tomatoes, cheese (swiss, feta, or parmesan ribbons), and hard-boiled egg slices.
- **Bean salad:** add citrus and lettuce; serve with corn chips.
- **Fruit salad:** spring greens with fruits—a fan shape of pear or apple slices combining red and green creates a beautiful salad; warm caramelized peach or pear slices are delicious on a bed of cool greens, served with nuts (raw, roasted or sugared); other delicious salad fruits in-

clude mandarin oranges, persimmons, berries, raisins, or craisins. Cheeses—parmesan chunks or ribbons (with vegetable peeler), feta, gorgonzola. Optional additions—chopped chicken, turkey, ham, bacon.

WARM QUINOA SALAD

1   Preheat oven to 400 degrees. In a saucepan, heat 1 tablespoon of olive oil.

2   Add 1 1/2 cups quinoa. Stir over medium heat for 2 minutes.

3   Add 3 cups water, salt, and vegetables of choice. Bring to a boil.

4   Cover and simmer for 15 minutes. Toss in apples and greens such as spinach or kale until apples are warm and greens are wilted. Serve warm.

DRESSINGS

OIL & VINEGAR DRESSINGS

- Choose a favorite oil and a favorite vinegar and mix them in equal parts or to your palate's delight!
- Use just a flavored oil OR a flavored vinegar on its own to dress your salad.
- Another simple and delicious combination is equal parts olive oil, red wine vinegar, and pure maple syrup.

RASPBERRY VINAIGRETTE

Makes 3/4 cup

- 2 tablespoons balsamic vinegar
- 1/2 cup fresh raspberries, mashed
- 1 tablespoon minced shallots
- 1/2 teaspoon dijon mustard
- 1/4 teaspoon salt
- Freshly ground black pepper
- 6 tablespoons olive oil

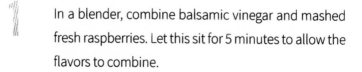 In a blender, combine balsamic vinegar and mashed fresh raspberries. Let this sit for 5 minutes to allow the flavors to combine.

LORI'S SALAD DRESSINGS

"I make my own salad dressings. I like knowing what's in my food and using fresh, raw ingredients. I go crazy in these shops that are popping up everywhere selling oils and vinegars on tap. I've brought samples home from New York, Portland, Salt Lake City, and Arizona. I have quite a collection! Besides their unique and attractive flavors, balsamic vinegars are said to aid digestion and weight loss, prevent fatigue, strengthen bones, and offer a number of antiviral and antibacterial properties."

2. Strain mixture, pressing hard to extract all the juice (to equal 1/4 cup).

3. Add the rest of the ingredients to the juice and whisk. Store in the fridge up to 2 weeks.

CITRUS BALSAMIC DRESSING

Makes about 2 cups

- 1/4 cup balsamic vinegar
- 3 peeled oranges
- 1/2 peeled lime
- Whites of 3 green onions
- 1 garlic clove
- 2 tablespoons raw honey
- Pinch of white pepper
- 1/2 teaspoon salt
- 1/2 cup olive oil

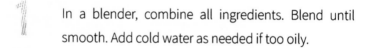 In a blender, combine all ingredients. Blend until smooth. Add cold water as needed if too oily.

BLEU CHEESE DRESSING

Makes 1 1/2 cups

- 1 cup Delicious 30-Second Homemade Mayonnaise (see page 41)
- 1 1/2 tablespoons raw apple cider vinegar
- Pinch of dry mustard
- 1/4 teaspoon salt

- Dash of fresh finely ground black pepper
- 1/4 cup olive oil
- 2 tablespoons water
- 1/4 cup bleu cheese crumbles

1. In a blender, combine all ingredients except bleu cheese. Blend until smooth.

2. Add bleu cheese crumbles and spin blades a few seconds to incorporate.

RANCH DRESSING DRY MIX

Yields enough to make 24 batches of ranch salad dressing

- 1 cup dried parsley flakes
- 1/2 cup finely crushed saltine crackers (about 15)
- 1/2 cup dried minced onion
- 1/2 cup garlic salt
- 1/2 cup onion salt
- 1/4 cup garlic powder
- 1/4 cup onion powder
- 2 tablespoons dried dill weed

1. In a large bowl, combine all ingredients. Mix well and store in airtight container in a cool, dry place.

RANCH DRESSING

- 2 tablespoons prepared Ranch Dressing Dry Mix (see page 61)
- 2 cups Delicious 30-Second Homemade Mayonnaise (see page 41)
- 2 cups buttermilk

1. Whisk together prepared mix, mayonnaise, and buttermilk. Chill for 30 minutes before serving.

TIP: FOR A CILANTRO LIME RANCH DRESSING, ADD CHOPPED CILANTRO PLUS ZEST AND JUICE OF 1 LIME.

DINNER

TURKEY SCALLOPINI

- 1/4 cup whole wheat pastry flour
- 1/4 cup parmesan cheese, grated
- Dash of salt
- Dash of pepper
- 1/4 teaspoon savory
- 1 teaspoon rosemary and/or marjoram, or 1 teaspoon Italian seasoning
- 1 turkey breast, thinly sliced
- 1/2 cup plain yogurt, or 1 lightly beaten egg

1   Stir together the pastry flour, parmesan, and seasonings.

2   Dip the turkey slices, one at a time, in yogurt or egg. Coat with the prepared flour mix.

3   Sauté slices in a pan with butter or cooking oil. Serve with a salad, on a sandwich, or with a side of mixed vegetables.

PROSCIUTTO-TOSSED ANGEL HAIR

1. Cook angel hair per package instructions. Meanwhile, soften onions and mushrooms in a frying pan with strips of sweet pepper, peas, and garlic.

2. Stir in prosciutto. Cook 3–5 minutes and serve warm over drained pasta.

EGGROLL SUPPER

- 1 pound breakfast or Italian sausage, or 1 pound ground beef
- 1 onion, chopped
- 1 cup mushrooms, chopped
- 2 cups frozen vegetable mix
- Eggroll wraps

1. Preheat oven to 375 degrees.

2. Heat meat, onion, and mushrooms in a frying pan, about 4–5 minutes. In the last minute of cooking, add frozen vegetables.

3. Spoon cooked mixture into eggroll wraps. Fold wraps and place on a cookie sheet.

4. Bake for 3–4 minutes, then turn over and bake another 3-4 minutes. Serve immediately.

FRUITY GARDEN SLAW

Start with shredded cabbage mixed with sections of blood orange, mango, apple, persimmon and/or melon chunks, grapes, celery slices, toasted pecans, almond slivers, cashews, pistachios, walnuts, or pine nuts. Mix with plain or vanilla yogurt. Add chow mein noodles, or substitute noodles for shredded cabbage.

COUSCOUS APPLE BOWL

- Carrots, shredded
- Non-bleeding beets (white, gold, or chioggia), shredded
- 1 onion, minced
- 1 apple, cut into chunks
- 1 package couscous
- Cheese, to taste
- Optional herbs: summer savory, marjoram, tarragon, or rosemary

1. Place 1 cup of shredded vegetables and apple chunks per serving into a small saucepan with 1/2 cup of water per serving. Bring to a boil until tender (about 8 minutes without the lid on).

2. Meanwhile, cook the couscous (takes 5 minutes). Herbs may be added to the water before couscous is cooked if desired.

3. Mix couscous, remaining apple chunks, grated or crumbled cheese, and cooked vegetables and serve warm. Salt and pepper to taste.

SAUSAGE SKILLET

1. Brown breakfast or Italian sausage in a frying pan. In the last minute of cooking, add a frozen vegetable mix.

2. Serve alone or with tortilla chips. Ground beef can substituted for sausage.

HAM & CHEESE QUESADILLA

- 1 tortilla
- Salsa or marinara
- Melting cheese, grated or sliced, such as parmesan, mozzarella, or provolone
- Sweet peppers, diced
- Deli ham, thinly sliced

1. Spray a frying pan with oil. Place tortilla with a spread of salsa or marinara in the pan.

2. Add a sprinkle of cheese, diced sweet peppers, and ham. Cook over medium heat until the cheese is melted.

TIP: COOK ON MEDIUM-LOW HEAT TO MAKE A HAM & CHEESE ROLL!

PITA TACOS

1. Cook ground beef with refried beans and taco seasoning.

2. Add grated cheese, sour cream, and salsa and serve in lightly toasted pita bread halves.

PAN-GLAZED BASIL CHICKEN

- 2 chicken breasts
- 1 tablespoon coconut oil
- 2 tablespoons balsamic vinegar
- 1 tablespoon honey
- 2 tablespoons chopped fresh basil (or 2 teaspoons dried basil)

1. Salt and pepper chicken breasts and sauté with coconut oil.

2. Meanwhile, make the glaze: combine balsamic vinegar, honey, and basil. Serve with mixed vegetables.

DESSERTS & SNACKS

Fruit is nature's dessert! Serve fresh fruit after any meal for the healthiest dessert. Try fruits you've never tried before. Have fun with it.

STRAWBERRY SENSATION

1. Start with a simple bowl of fresh whole strawberries with stems removed.

2. Top with a dollop of honey-sweetened sour cream.

3. Sprinkle with a pinch of Chinese Five Spice.

FROZEN GRAPES

1. That's it! Frozen grapes! So refreshing, especially on a hot summer day.

LORI'S QUICK SORBET

If you have a masticating juicer (such as a Champion), you can make luscious sorbets in a jiffy by replacing the juicing screen with its solid counterpart.

- Frozen banana chunks (1–2 inches)—these are a must, because they bind the other fruits and make the sorbet creamy
- Other frozen fruits cut into pieces that will fit into the chute of your machine

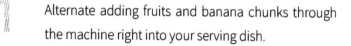 Alternate adding fruits and banana chunks through the machine right into your serving dish.

BLENDER METHOD: YOU CAN MAKE SORBET IN A BLENDER WITH FROZEN FRUIT; HOWEVER, YOU WILL NEED ENOUGH LIQUID TO COVER THE BLADES. TRY COCONUT WATER, RICE OR ALMOND MILK, STEVIA WATER, APPLE JUICE, OR ANY COMPLEMENTARY JUICE. YOU MAY WANT TO PUT THE BLENDED MIX IN THE FREEZER FOR A FEW MINUTES BEFORE SERVING.

TIP: YOU CAN USE BERRIES, BUT KNOW THAT YOU WILL GET SEEDS IN YOUR SORBET. BLUEBERRIES ARE BETTER LEFT OUT AS THEY TURN THE SORBET A GRAY COLOR WITH ANNOYING BITS OF SKIN.

MINT CHIP NICE CREAM

Makes approximately 5 cups

- 1 cup coconut water
- 1 cup pitted dates (10–11 dates)
- 2 handfuls fresh spinach (about 4 cups loosely packed)
- 1 handful fresh kale (optional)
- 1 avocado, pitted
- 1 teaspoon peppermint extract, or about 6 large fresh mint leaves
- 2 trays ice cubes (28 cubes)
- 1/2 cup dairy-free, soy-free mini chocolate chips

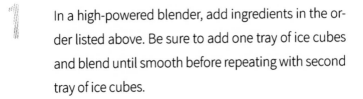 In a high-powered blender, add ingredients in the order listed above. Be sure to add one tray of ice cubes and blend until smooth before repeating with second tray of ice cubes.

2. Blend on high speed until smooth, using the blender plunger to incorporate. Taste and add more peppermint flavor or mint leaves if desired.

3. Blend again until smooth. Stir in chocolate chips. Serve immediately.

TIP: LEFTOVERS CAN BE FROZEN; HOWEVER, THE TEXTURE IS A BIT ICY. LET THAW A FEW MINUTES BEFORE SCOOPING. STILL VERY DELICIOUS!

GUILT-FREE SWEET POPCORN

- 1/3 cup coconut oil
- 1/3 cup raw honey
- 1 large bowl of air-popped popcorn

1. Combine coconut oil and raw honey in a saucepan over low heat and warm until melted.

2. Pour the warm mixture over the popcorn and toss to coat. The amounts of coconut oil and honey can be increased (in equal parts) to match the volume of popcorn.

EASY PEASY PINE NUT PUDDING

1. Add equal measurements of water (or coconut water), chopped pitted dates, and raw or lightly toasted pine nuts to a high speed blender and puree until creamy.

2. Spoon into dessert dishes and sprinkle with a few raw pine nuts and a pinch of cinnamon if desired. A surprisingly simple and delicious quick dessert!

TIP: DELICIOUS MADE WITH CASHEWS OR MACADAMIAS!

SIMPLE CHIA SEED PUDDING

- 2 cups vanilla almond milk (or milk of your choice)
- 1/3 cup chia seeds (use 1/2 cup for a thicker pudding)
- 1 tablespoon maple syrup (or sweetener of choice)
- 1 teaspoon vanilla (optional)

1. Whisk ingredients together by hand. Let stand for two minutes so the chia seeds can begin to soften.

2   Whisk again (to prevent clumping) and let stand for
    two more minutes.

3   Repeat five more times. Chill in the refrigerator. Serve
    plain or with berries.

TIP: ADD 1 TEASPOON RAW CACAO POWDER AND AN-
OTHER TEASPOON OF SWEETENER FOR CHOCOLATE
CHIA SEED PUDDING.

BALSAMIC SPARKLING BEVERAGES

1   To a glass of club soda or sparkling water, add a large
    drizzle of a flavored artisan balsamic vinegar. Stir to
    mix.

TIP: THESE ARE SOME OF OUR FAVORITE VINEGARS: VA-
NILLA FIG, HONEY DATE, JUNIPER BERRY, WHITE CO-
CONUT LIME, BLACK CHERRY, CRANBERRY PEAR, CIN-
NAMON PEAR, DARK CHOCOLATE.

QUICK APPLE CRISP

1. Preheat oven to 350 degrees. Butter a baking dish or individual oven-proof serving dishes.

2. Add sliced or diced organic apples. Sprinkle lightly with coconut palm sugar.

3. Top with granola (see page 76) and a drizzle of pure maple syrup.

4. Bake for 15 minutes or until apples are done to desired tenderness.

LORI'S FAVORITE HOMEMADE GRANOLA

Okay, so this takes more than 15 minutes to prepare! BUT, once made, it's ready for preparing a meal or snack in UNDER ONE MINUTE!

- 4 cups rolled oats (Lori rolls her own oats so they are fresh and aromatic!)
- 1 1/2 cups chopped nuts
- 1/2 cup unsweetened coconut
- 1/2 cup coconut oil
- 3/4 cup raw honey
- 1 teaspoon pure vanilla

1   Preheat oven to 300 degrees. In a large bowl, combine oats, nuts, and unsweetened coconut.

2   Melt oil and honey over low heat until combined, and then add vanilla. Pour half of the honey mixture over the oat mixture and stir well.

3   Spread oat mixture on a baking sheet and bake for 10 minutes. Stir oats and drizzle remaining honey mixture over oat mixture.

4   Bake 10–15 minutes more. Let cool on baking sheet.

5   When cool, add dried fruit pieces and orange or lemon zest. Cover tightly and store in the refrigerator.

TIP: THIS IS DELICIOUS ON HOMEMADE NO-COOK VIILI YOGURT WITH BERRIES (SEE SEEDRENAISSANCE. COM FOR YOGURT INFORMATION), ON ICE CREAM, AS A CEREAL WITH ALMOND MILK, AS A TOPPING FOR APPLE CRISP OR A BOWL OF FRESH FRUIT, OR JUST PLAIN AS A SNACK!

THE HIVE MIND SPEAKS: 15-MINUTE MEAL IDEAS

Turning to a group of friends and family online—a hive mind—I asked my hundreds of Facebook and website followers to weigh in with their "go-to" meals, the healthy, mindful meals they rely on regularly for a quick family meal. Hundreds of people—men, women, and college students—responded, and the results were intriguing and useful. We wanted to include these here not because this list is groundbreaking or "new" information but simply because both of the authors find it helpful to keep a list of time-tested ideas. That way, when your family is hungry and time is short, you'll have an at-a-glance list of quick ideas that can be made from scratch, with healthy and mindful ingredients, in 15 minutes or less.

Here are some of their ideas:

STIR-FRY

Far and away the winner online, many people said they often turn to this favorite when pinched for time. Protein suggestions ranged from adding chicken, pork, sliced steak, shrimp, fish, tofu, or any of the vegetarian protein foods now available. Almost everyone said they add whatever vegetables are easily available in their gardens and fridges, ranging from roots to greens to corn and other grains. Some people served this over white rice, some over the healthier brown rice option, some used a combo, and some put it over quinoa or a seed mix or ate the vegetables and protein without putting it over a grain. Others suggested marinated meat (with any number of marinades) with steamed vegetables, stir-fried, or over rice. Others suggested variations on chow mein or rice noodles.

A couple people suggested (and even posted pictures) that the new "hot" food trend is to use larvae or bugs or something as your protein. (I'll pass on that trend! When you ask the Internet to weigh in, you have to be prepared for anything!)

PASTAS AND GRAINS

VENETIAN PASTA

1   Cook shaped pasta or noodles with sliced onion.

2   Drizzle on olive oil and balsamic vinegar.

3   Sprinkle white raisins, capers (optional), toasted pine nuts, and spinach.

SIMILAR IDEAS:

- Pasta of choice with seasoned ground beef and onions, mixed with spaghetti sauce, frozen mixed vegetables, and grated cheese
- Linguine with sautéed vegetables including carrots, sweet peppers, zucchini, garlic, and Italian seasoning with a white or marinara sauce
- Prepared ravioli with zucchini, parmesan, and sage
- Penne or other shaped pasta with steak strips, kale, melted butter, gorgonzola, and salt and pepper
- Lemon juice–flavored spaghetti with spinach and sausage
- Spaghetti
- Couscous with diced tomatoes, salsa, and meat (if desired)

- Couscous with meat and vegetables
- Couscous with zucchini, lemon, thyme, vegetables, and meat (if desired)
- Couscous with steamed cauliflower and white sauce

TACOS

Many people online said they turn to tacos for a fast meal. Some use homemade taco seasoning (see page 42), and some use prepared seasoning. Some use refried beans (I am partial to this) with taco meat, and some use shredded cabbage instead of lettuce. Some people top with salsa, some with ketchup.

SANDWICHES AND WRAPS

CHICKPEA BURGERS

- 1 15-oz can garbanzo beans (chickpeas)
- 1/3 cup thick natural yeast (Click on "Yeasts and Cultures" at SeedRenaissance.com for details)
- 1 1/2 teaspoon all-natural organic beef bouillon powder
- 1/2 onion, chopped
- 1/4 teaspoon savory

- 1/4 teaspoon salt
- 1/2 teaspoon chili powder
- 1/8 teaspoon ground clove
- 1/4 teaspoon paprika
- 1 1/2 tablespoons olive oil
- 1/3 cup parmesan (optional)
- 1 tablespoon additional olive oil (to cook patties)

1. Incorporate all ingredients and form burgers with your hands.

2. Cook in a skillet on medium heat. Serve warm.

SIMILAR IDEAS:

- Dolmas (Dolmas were new to me. These are grape or cabbage leaves stuffed with meat and/or vegetables and can be purchased, prepared, and put into a wrap or sandwich or eaten on their own.)
- Barbecue chicken or pork wraps
- Curry chicken salad with dried cranberries and sprouts on pita
- Black bean quesadillas or pinto or refried beans with cheese and prepared taco meat

- Crab rolls

- Burritos

- Turkey or beef spinach sliders

- Peanut butter sandwiches: Elvis style, classic, or with honey or stevia (see my cookbook, *The Stevia Solution*)

- Kabobs (many options of vegetables, meats, fruits, marinades, and glazes)

- Savory crepes with deli meat, cheese, and a side salad

ONE OF MY AND LORI'S ALL-TIME FAVORITES IS A SIMPLE CHEESE, FRUIT, AND NUT PLATE.

BOWLS AND SLAWS

Food bowls are an emerging food trend, often with Greek, Brazilian, or other flavors. However, my online friends said they most often turned to something more simple: a chicken rice bowl. They suggested mixing about 1 cup of mixed vegetables with shredded chicken over brown rice. Others suggested sautéing ground turkey or beef with shredded cabbage and carrots or a raw package of coleslaw mix, flavored with garlic, ginger, soy, rice wine vinegar, and sesame oil.

NO-COOK APPLE SLAW WITH MEAT

- 1 teaspoon olive oil
- 1 cubed red apple
- 4–6 cups Chinese cabbage or bok choy
- 1 onion, sliced
- 1/3 cup plain yogurt (I prefer homemade viili; see my book *Viili Perpetual No-Cook Homemade Yogurt* for details)
- Chopped pepperoni, salami, or deli meat to taste
- 2 tablespoons fresh lemon juice
- Salt and pepper to taste

 Mix all ingredients together.

WINTER SLAW

- 2 tablespoons lemon juice
- 1/4 cabbage, shredded
- 6–8 brussels sprouts
- Pecans to taste
- Deli meat or bacon to taste
- Optional: a drizzle of balsamic vinegar and a touch of honey

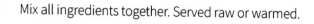 Mix all ingredients together. Served raw or warmed.

SIMILAR IDEAS:

- Parsnip hash: chopped parsnips, potatoes, and mixed vegetables with colorful sweet peppers and onions and your choice of meat
- Deli ham, fresh or canned corn, lettuce, and croutons, tossed; serve with cantaloupe and dressing
- Nachos: I prefer sweet pork topped with mozzarella and lots of romaine lettuce, drizzled generously with lime juice

PIZZA

CHILI PIZZAS

1   Preheat oven to 400 degrees. Spread flour tortillas over a cookie sheet.

2   Top with a thick chili, shredded cheese, and black olives.

3   Bake for 5–10 minutes or until cheese is melted.

EGGS

POTATOES O'BRIEN

1. Pan-fry sliced potatoes with colorful bell peppers.

2. Serve warm. Scrambled eggs can be added if desired.

WILTED GREENS

1. Melt lard or bacon grease in a skillet (or cook a couple strips of bacon per serving).

2. Sauté onions with garlic.

3. Wilt Swiss chard, collard greens, or other greens. Remove to a plate.

4. Cook an egg over easy (I prefer over hard). Place egg with the wilted greens and squeeze fresh lemon juice (I prefer lime juice).

- Frittatas with onions and summer savory or marjoram
- Fried or scrambled eggs with cumin, spinach, and tomatoes
- Hard-boiled eggs with curry powder, garbanzo beans or peas, and fresh herbs such as parsley, marjoram, or tarragon

MEATS AND VEGETABLES

SAMPLE IDEAS:

- Marinated or dry-rubbed meats with mixed vegetables
- White fish cooked with lime juice and a Chinese five-spice blend
- Steak and green beans with potatoes or mixed vegetables
- Scallops with corn, avocado, mixed vegetables, and lime juice
- Ham steak with steamed vegetables
- Pork chops with a salad
- Spiral-cut vegetables (using a home spiralizing tool such as a Veggetti) with salt and herb dressing with cheese; serve raw or sauté with coconut oil

VEGETABLES, FRUITS, BERRIES & HERBS

GUIDE TO HEALTHY NUTRIENTS

All data is US Department of Agriculture data
unless otherwise noted.

One of the recurring problems with trying to eat mindfully is that finding reliable scientific nutrition information about basic ingredients can be difficult. Compiling this list took many hours, but Lori and I feel that this information empowers people who are looking to eat mindfully. Nutrition is the key to health, and nutrition is only found in whole, real foods.

VEGETABLES

- **Asparagus** contains 1% of your daily value of dietary fiber, 2% vitamin A, 1% vitamin C, and 1% iron.

- **Beans** are a powerhouse of nutrition, providing 100% of your daily value of dietary fiber, 78% protein, 70% potassium, 62% magnesium, 54% iron, 35% vitamin B6, and 13% calcium!

- **Beets** are an excellent source of folate (natural folic acid, a form of vitamin B) and a good source of manganese. According to the Mayo Clinic website, folic acid helps women of childbearing age prevent specific kinds of birth defects. Folic acid is also of interest with respect to cognitive enhancement, cancer, psychiatric illnesses, and cardiovascular conditions. Manganese, according to Oregon State University's Micronutrient Information Center, is essential for cellular antioxidant function, metabolism, bone development, and wound healing.

- **Broccoli** contains 13% of your daily value of potassium, 15% dietary fiber, 8% protein, 18% vitamin A, 7% calcium, 220% vitamin C, 6% iron, 15% vitamin B6, and 7% magnesium.

- **Brussels sprouts** contain 9% of your daily value of potassium, 13% dietary fiber, 6% protein, 13% vitamin A, 3%

calcium, 124% vitamin C, 6% iron, 10% vitamin B6, and 5% magnesium.

- **Cabbage** contains 1% of your daily value of potassium, 2% dietary fiber, and 14% vitamin C.
- **Cantaloupe** contains 42% of your daily value of potassium, 20% dietary fiber, 9% protein, 373% vitamin A, 5% calcium, 337% vitamin C, 6% iron, 20% vitamin B6, and 16% magnesium.
- **Carrots** are a great source of potassium (7%), dietary fiber (8%), vitamin A (110%), vitamin C (10%), calcium (2%), and iron (2%), according to US FDA studies.
- **Cauliflower** contains 50% of your daily value of potassium, 48% dietary fiber, 22% protein, 12% calcium, 472% vitamin C, 13% iron, 55% vitamin B6, and 22% magnesium.
- **Celeriac** contains 13% of your daily value of potassium, 11% dietary fiber, 4% protein, 6% calcium, 20% vitamin C, 6% iron, 15% vitamin B6, and 7% magnesium.
- **Corn** contains 13% of the daily recommended value of potassium, 32% protein, 1% calcium, 25% iron, 50% vitamin B6, and 52% magnesium.
- **Cucumbers** contain 2% of your daily value of potassium, 1% dietary fiber, 1% vitamin A, 2% vitamin C, and 1% magnesium.
- **Eggplant** contains 5% of your daily value of potassium,

10% dietary fiber, 1% protein, 3% vitamin C, 1% iron, 5% vitamin B6, and 2% magnesium.

- **Garlic** contains 1% of your daily value of vitamin C.
- **Honeydew melon** contains 8% of your daily value of potassium, 4% dietary fiber, 1% protein, 1% vitamin A, 40% vitamin C, 1% iron, 5% vitamin B6, and 3% magnesium.
- **Kale** contains 9% of your daily value of potassium, 5% protein, 133% vitamin A, 10% calcium, 134% vitamin C, 5% iron, 10% vitamin B6, and 7% magnesium.
- **Leeks** contain 2% of your daily value of vitamin A and 1% vitamin C.
- **Lettuce** provides 130% of your daily value of vitamin A, 6% vitamin C, 5% potassium, 4% dietary fiber, 4% iron, and 2% calcium.
- **Onions** contain 4% of your daily value of potassium, 7% dietary fiber, 2% protein, 13% vitamin C, 2% calcium, 1% iron, 5% vitamin B6, and 2% magnesium.
- **Parsnips** contain 14% of your daily value of potassium, 28% dietary fiber, 3% protein, 4% calcium, 37% vitamin C, 4% iron, 5% vitamin B6, and 9% magnesium.
- **Peas** provide a whopping 96% of your daily value of vitamin C, 28% dietary fiber, 10% potassium, 16% protein, 11% iron, 10% vitamin B6, 11% magnesium, 3% calcium, and 22% vitamin A.

- **Peppers** contain an astonishing 190% of your daily value of vitamin C! They also contain 8% of your dietary fiber, 6% potassium, 2% Vitamin A, 4% calcium, and 4% iron.

- **Potatoes** contain 25% of your daily value of potassium, 18% dietary fiber, 8% protein, 2% calcium, 70% vitamin C, 9% iron, 30% vitamin B6, and 12% magnesium.

- **Pumpkin**: With 197% of your daily value of vitamin A, pumpkin is a powerhouse for health! Pumpkin also contains 17% of your vitamin C, 11% potassium, 4% iron, 5% vitamin B6, 2% calcium, 2% dietary fiber, 2% protein, and 3% magnesium!

- **Rutabaga** contains 33% of your daily value of vitamin C, 9% iron, 20% vitamin B6, 19% magnesium, 16% calcium, 33% potassium, 36% dietary fiber, and 8% protein.

- **Soybeans** contain 95% of your daily value of potassium, 68% dietary fiber, 136% protein, 51% calcium, 18% vitamin C, 162% iron, 35% vitamin B6, and 130% magnesium.

- **Spinach** is a great source of vitamin A (56%), vitamin C (14%), iron (4%), calcium (3%), vitamin B6 (5%), magnesium (6%), potassium (4%), and dietary fiber (2%).

- **Tomatoes** provide potassium (10%), dietary fiber (4%), vitamin A (40%), vitamin C (20%), calcium (2%), and iron (4%).

- **Turnips** contain 42% of your daily value of vitamin C, 8%

dietary fiber, 6% potassium, 5% vitamin B6, 3% calcium, 3% magnesium, and 2% iron.

- **Watermelon** contains 8% of your daily value of potassium, 4% dietary fiber, 3% protein, 31% vitamin A, 2% calcium, 37% vitamin C, 3% iron, 5% vitamin B6, and 7% magnesium.

- **Wheat** contains 23% of your daily value of potassium, 52% protein, 6% calcium, 37% iron, 40% vitamin B6, and 69% magnesium.

- **Zucchini** contains 30% of your daily value of vitamin C, 6% vitamin A, 7% potassium, 2% iron, 5% Vitamin B6, 2% calcium, and 8% dietary fiber (USDA data).

FRUITS & BERRIES

- **Apples** contain 5% of your daily value of potassium, 17% dietary fiber, 1% protein, 1% vitamin A, 1% calcium, 14% vitamin C, 1% iron, 5% vitamin B6, and 2% magnesium.

- **Avocado** contains 20% of your daily value of potassium, 40% dietary fiber, 5% protein, 4% vitamin A, 1% calcium, 24% vitamin C, 4% iron, 20% vitamin B6, and 10% magnesium.

- **Bananas** contain 12% of your daily value of potassium, 12% dietary fiber, 2% protein, 1% vitamin A, 17% vitamin C, 1% iron, 20% vitamin B6, and 8% magnesium.

- **Blackberries** contain 6% of your daily value of potassium, 32% dietary fiber, 4% protein, 6% vitamin A, 4% calcium, 50% vitamin C, 4% iron, and 7% magnesium.

- **Grapes** contain 5% of your daily value of potassium, 3% dietary fiber, 1% protein, 6% vitamin C, 1% iron, 5% vitamin B6, 1% magnesium, 1% vitamin A, and 1% calcium.

- **Mangoes** contain 16% of your daily value of potassium, 20% dietary fiber, 5% protein, 72% vitamin A, 3% calcium, 203% vitamin C, 2% iron, 20% vitamin B6, and 8% magnesium.

- **Peaches** contain 8% of your daily value of potassium, 9% dietary fiber, 2% protein, 9% vitamin A, 16% vitamin C, 2% iron, and 3% magnesium.

- **Pears** contain 5% of your daily value of potassium, 24% dietary fiber, 1% protein, 12% vitamin C, 1% calcium, 1% iron, 5% vitamin B6, and 3% magnesium.

- **Pineapple** contains 28% of your daily value of potassium, 52% dietary fiber, 9% protein, 10% vitamin A, 11% calcium, 721% vitamin C, 14% iron, 50% vitamin B6, and 27% magnesium.

- **Strawberries** are a fantastic source of Vitamin C (160% of your daily value) and also a source of potassium*, iron, calcium, and dietary fiber, according to US FDA studies.

*Potassium is a critical daily nutrient for maintenance of cell membranes, enzyme production, avoiding hypokalemia, and prevention of stroke, osteoporosis, kidney stones, and high blood pressure, according to Oregon State University's Micronutrient Information Center.

HERBS

- **Basil** contains 5% of your daily value of vitamin A, 1% vitamin C, and 1% iron.

- **Chives** contain 2% of your daily value of vitamin A and 2% vitamin C.

- **Cinnamon** contains 16% of your daily value of dietary fiber, 3% iron, 1% magnesium, and 7% calcium.

- **Coriander** contains 5% of your daily value of vitamin A and 1% vitamin C.

- **Cumin** contains 3% of your daily value of potassium, 2% dietary fiber, 2% protein, 1% vitamin A, 5% calcium, 22% iron, and 5% magnesium.

- **Fennel** contains 10% of your daily value of potassium, 10% dietary fiber, 2% protein, 2% vitamin A, 4% calcium, 17% vitamin C, 3% iron, and 3% magnesium.

- **Ginger** contains 1% of your daily value of potassium, 1% vitamin C, and 1% magnesium.

- **Oregano** contains 3% of your daily value of dietary fiber, 2% calcium, 3% iron, and 1% magnesium.
- **Parsley** contains 8% of your daily value of vitamin C, 6% vitamin A, and 1% iron.
- **Rosemary** contains 1% of your daily value of vitamin A.
- **Tarragon** contains 4% of your daily value of potassium, 1% dietary fiber, 2% protein, 4% vitamin A, 5% calcium, 4% vitamin C, 8% iron, 5% vitamin B6, and 4% magnesium.
- **Thyme** contains 2% of your daily value of vitamin C.

DO YOU HAVE A FAVORITE 15-MINUTE MINDFUL RECIPE THAT YOU DON'T SEE IN THIS BOOK? SHARE IT WITH US! EMAIL YOUR FEEDBACK TO CALEBWARNOCK@YAHOO.COM.

FREE OFFER: GET A FREE PACKAGE OF HEIRLOOM VEGETABLE SEEDS OR A NATURAL YEAST STARTER AT SEEDRENAISSANCE.COM TODAY BY VISITING THE WEBSITE AND CLICKING ON THE "FREE OFFERS" TAB!

ABOUT THE AUTHORS

Caleb Warnock is the popular author of the Backyard Renaissance collection of books as well as *Forgotten Skills of Self-Sufficiency Used by the Mormon Pioneers*, *The Art of Baking with Natural Yeast*, *Backyard Winter Gardening for All Climates*, *More Forgotten Skills*, *Trouble's On The Menu*, and more. He is the owner of SeedRenaissance.com. You can find his instructional YouTube videos by searching "YouTube Caleb Warnock" on Google. Join the author's email list by going to SeedRenaissance.com and finding the "Join The List" section in the bottom left-hand corner of the homepage.

Lori Henderson has worked for many years in the broadcasting industry as an executive assistant in Salt Lake City, Utah. Recently, she has partnered with her husband, Matt Henderson, in the creation of MormonMediaNetwork.com, a group of websites including MormonHippie.com (holistic and self-reliant living), featuring Caleb Warnock's internet radio program "Forgotten Skills Radio" and conversations with Caleb on their internet radio program "Mormon Tea." Lori has four children and three grandchildren. She loves yoga and tai chi, meditation, gardening, earthing, traveling, tea parties, and studying and advocating health and wellness through holistic living. Lori is a certified energy healing practitioner and has training in the use of medicinal herbs, essential oils, and aromatherapy. She says, "Our prescription for happy, healthy living is wholesome foods and herbs, recreation and exercise, and positive thinking and thankfulness." Learn more about Lori at TurningHeartsTogether.com.

ABOUT FAMILIUS

VISIT OUR WEBSITE: www.familius.com

JOIN OUR FAMILY: There are lots of ways to connect with us! Subscribe to our newsletters at www.familius.com to receive uplifting daily inspiration, essays from our Pater Familius, a free ebook every month, and the first word on special discounts and Familius news.

GET BULK DISCOUNTS: If you feel a few friends and family might benefit from what you've read, let us know and we'll be happy to provide you with quantity discounts. Simply email us at specialorders@familius.com.

CONNECT:

www.facebook.com/paterfamilius

@familiustalk, @paterfamilius1

www.pinterest.com/familius

THE MOST IMPORTANT WORK YOU EVER DO WILL BE WITHIN THE WALLS OF YOUR OWN HOME.

CPSIA information can be obtained
at www.ICGtesting.com
Printed in the USA
LVOW12s0055290816

502056LV00001B/2/P